CULTIVATE

LOOK, LIVE, LOVE LIKE JESUS

A DISCIPLESHIP TRAINING PROGRAM FOR WOMEN

(PART 1)

SAMANTHA MILLER

Cultivate: Look, Live, Love Like Jesus

Published by All Peoples Ministries
727 Old Graves Mill Road
Lynchburg, Virginia 24502
www.allpeoplesministries.org

Cover and Interior design by Samuel C. Petty

ISBN: 978-1-961983-03-8

Printed in the United States of America

ACKNOWLEDGEMENTS

We honor Pastor Jeff Crawford and All Peoples Ministries for believing in our mission and investing in the future of developing young women.

CONTENTS

The goals of this curriculum are three-fold:

1. Know the Word of God and the doctrines of faith.

2. Gather to develop lasting Christ-focused relationships.

3. Fully embody the image of Christ through discipleship.

HOW TO USE THIS CURRICULUM

Cultivate is a set of curricula designed to help women thrive in a healthy spiritual formation and live in the realities of present kingdom lifestyle. Therefore, the goals of this curriculum are three -fold: that women would come to know the Word of God and the doctrines of faith, that women would gather to develop lasting Christ-focused relationships, and that women would fully embody the image of Christ through discipleship.

Each curriculum covers specific doctrinal topics that are essential in spiritual formation. Most of our curriculum is designed to be non-denominational and merely a guide for women to have the tools to read and understand Scripture themselves and to learn from one another. The authors believe our faith should be rooted in our relationships with the Triune God and the Word of the Holy Scriptures. We are happy to be guides but never replace personal faith. No preacher, teacher, curriculum, or Christian influencer should replace an individual pursuit of Christ.

Each lesson is designed to:

- Introduce a topic
- Give basic knowledge about the subject
- Provide scripture references to support the topic
- Provide individual and group-based questions and activities.

Another important aspect of this curriculum is that it was written to be as comprehensive as possible while leaving room for the leader and the participants to use their gifts. The teachers in the groups should study beforehand and be ready to contribute by providing more meat, stories, Scripture, and application. The intercessors or pastors of the group should feel free to feel the flow of the Spirit, so that women are praying for each other, listening to each other, and ministering to each other. Do what is on the page but then go beyond it to match the unique needs of your group. We would be honored to hear your suggestions or testimonies about how this worked for you!

There is no designated time estimate for completing each curriculum or each lesson. As this curriculum was developed and tested, 45 minutes or more was essential for fostering meaningful engagement with the materials. However, proceed at a pace that you and the group deem necessary to complete each section. We would also recommend pairing the

How to Use this Curriculum

Introduction with the first lesson for optimal content preparation. Additionally, the final few sections of the last unit are longer than normal. It may be helpful to evaluate the group size to determine how many sessions to allocate to those sections. Remember, imposing a time limit on these lessons may disrupt what the Spirit wants to do, so we encourage you to be flexible; if that means one lesson must go into another week, so be it!

We are so excited for you to use these curricula to grow in an intentional community with women who want to look more like Jesus and love one another like Jesus.

INTRODUCTION

INTRODUCTION

As I sit to write this introduction, I am experiencing one of the lowest moments in my spiritual journey of discipleship. I am staring at the reality of discipleship gone wrong. A woman I once walked with several years ago in discipleship has publicly denounced Christianity. Some of the fault is my own, and some belongs to others. This news is fresh, and there have been moments over the last few days when I considered throwing this entire work in the trash and forfeiting discipleship altogether.

Truth be told, I began working on this curriculum three years ago in response to the Lord calling me to find a Biblical model of discipleship after having a poor one modeled to me that, in turn, caused me to disciple wrongly in certain instances. I made emotional decisions in those rare occurrences when discipleship became hard and ended up hurting people because I had no solid footing on what a relationship like this should look like. I loved people deeply, and there was never ill intention, but I lacked wisdom. Yet I knew it was part of the Christian walk to disciple and be in discipleship myself. There must be a way to do this right. I didn't want a man's model, after all man's models had failed me – I only wanted Jesus' model.

I have taken so long to establish this curriculum because, to be quite honest, I didn't want to mess this up. I wanted to work through it with trusted friends and girls that I've mentored. I wanted to test it, and I wanted to live it out. I wanted to be transformed by it personally. I grieve over my part in hurting people through discipleship, and I grieve over the continual stories of church hurt and spiritual abuse that I listen to daily. I also grieve that as I look around me at churches all over the world and even in the Christian university that I teach and see that so many Christians are living a life that does not look like Jesus when the tools to do so are right in front of our face in the Word of God. I grieve that intentional Christ-like relationships outside and even through social media are a rarity in our modern culture. Despite this grief, I know that I serve a God who redeems and restores. I asked Him to use my brokenness and mistakes and turn them into good for His glory.

Perhaps my admission of fault in this area may disqualify me in your mind from writing a curriculum on this topic. After all, if someone is writing a book about a topic of spiritual formation, they must certainly be an expert. I have just confessed that I have failed at the very thing I am writing about. I can understand that it might be hard to trust the words in this curriculum because of this. Trust is something that is earned. By airing all my dirty laundry, I have a job to do. But – I committed that I would not do this job alone. This curriculum has contributors who have not only held me accountable as I have grown and recovered from some mess-ups in this area, but also contributors who are equally committed to seeing discipleship be rightfully understood and executed because there are lives at stake.

So, grab some friends, brew some coffee, eat some snacks, and get real with us in this curriculum as we pursue the likeness of Jesus. Consider allowing the words in this curriculum to generate conversations that might progress not just your own spiritual development but the spiritual development of others. It will be even better if you make a lifelong friend or two.

PART 1:

CULTIVATING THE SOIL

Discipleship Jesus' Way

LESSON 1 – CULTIVATE

Relationships are at the center of our very existence. We were conceived because a man and a woman came together in an intimate relational experience with one another. We learned to walk and talk through watching and interacting with our parents or caregivers. Our morals and values are usually formed from our relationships with our parents and loved ones. God created us with his very breath (Genesis 2:7) to be in a relationship with Him, and it delighted Him to favor humanity and entrust us with authority on earth (Genesis 1:26-30).

From this initial desire to be in relationship with His creation, relationships with God and one another become a foundational aspect of Christian living (Genesis 2:18). Relationships were so valuable to God that once sin separated us from Him, He did the only thing possible to restore relationship – He bore it for us. The Lord came to earth as a man, lived a perfect life, then gave His life to pay the penalty for our choice to choose sin over eternal relationship and restore what had been broken. So yes, this relationship thing is a big deal.

Defining relationships

Relationships are, by nature, connections between two or more people. Scripture defines and describes various types of relationships. There are more intimate relationships, such as marriage, friendship, and that between a parent and a child. The other types of relationships are less intimate and more authority-driven, such as between a ruler and His subjects or even a church leader and those they shepherd. Regardless of the circumstances of that connection, all relationships require effort from all parties involved, and it's not always easy. Although the initial design for relationship was to be a blessing to humanity, it does not always work out that way. It is time to change that, and it starts with us.

QUESTIONS FOR DISCUSSION

How have certain relationships in your life, for better or worse, impacted your physical, mental, and spiritual health?

What does it mean to you to cultivate a relationship?

To cultivate something is to improve, nurture, or develop something through care or attention. How can this definition be applied to the relationships in your life? What does it say about the time/intention required for certain relationships?

LESSON 2 – A HARD LOOK AT DISCIPLESHIP

Discipleship, an important biblical form of relationship, is a buzzword in Christianity that needs to be better understood and handled. Jesus calls us to make disciples, so there must be a way for the church to do this well. A good look at scripture reveals the truth about discipleship and why this relationship matters.

- Discipleship can be defined as the process through which a person is conformed into the image of Christ. (John 13:15-17 and 1 Corinthians 11:1)
- Discipleship was created and established by Jesus Himself; therefore, discipleship should always be rooted in relationship. (John 15)
- Discipleship occurs through a personal relationship with the Godhead and through developing relationships with mature believers in the body of Christ. ((John 14-16 and Ephesians 4:11-17)
- The purpose of discipleship is to make more followers of Jesus who look like Jesus, not followers of any other man, ministry, or religion. (Romans 8:29)
- To disciple is to teach others to submit to the Lord and obey His commands by abiding (trusting) in Him and Him alone, not through striving or legalistic standards. (John 8:31-32)
- If any aspect of a relationship doesn't model Jesus, it is counterfeit! (1Corinthians 11:1)
- Discipleship is costly, as we are called to share in the fellowship of Christ's suffering (2 Corinthians 4:17, Luke 9:23).

The point of this curriculum is not to give you man's ideas of discipleship but to instead focus on God's principles for discipleship, as evidenced in His Word. Man's ideas fail, but God's principles prevail. So, what does God tell us about discipleship? This curriculum will not only define discipleship but also thoroughly address various aspects of it to help us cultivate healthy and thriving relationships within the realm of discipleship.

CRITICAL THINKING AND DISCUSSION

What is discipleship?

Why is discipleship important?

Where does discipleship happen?

Lesson 2 | A Hard Look at Discipleship

When does discipleship start?

How can it happen well?

LESSON 3 – TEAM JESUS

To quote our pastor, *"We want God's ideas, not just good ideas."* Jesus must be the model for everything we do, say, and think.

Kingdom work is a family affair when you are a child of God. We join a "team" when we enter a relationship and community via discipleship, whether by joining a church, a small group community, or mentorship.

Critical Thinking Exercise:

Consider an athletic team and evaluate the team members' different roles. How do these roles transfer to "Team Jesus" members, specifically when considering discipleship?

Head Coach- Jesus

Team Captains - those discipling (mature disciples)

Team Members- those being discipled

As with any team, there is one head coach—Jesus. However, in Kingdom work, the game has already been won, and through discipleship, we are the vessels through which Jesus' name and victory are shared. Through Jesus, discipleship became the pathway for the "Great Commission."

Exploring Scripture Exercise:

Spend time digesting the Scripture quoted as the "Great Commission" from Matthew 28:16-20.

As you do this, consider the following important aspects for reading and understanding Scripture:

Who was the audience?

What is the context (where is Jesus, and what are the circumstances)?

What did this mean to the audience?

How does this apply today without changing the text's original meaning?

The Great Commission calls us to recruit more team members and train them in the ways of the Kingdom. These people do the discipling or are the "team captains."

Now, consider the following question:

According to this Scripture, what is the job description of the head coach? the team captain? the team members?

In teaching His disciples, Jesus showed them how to teach others. To be taught, you must submit to those teaching you and display a teachable spirit. In addition, the team captains never graduate from being discipled or remove themselves from accountability (more on this later.) **Submission to the ways of Christ is the primary qualification to enter discipleship, either as the one who is discipling or the one who is being discipled.** Remember, Jesus would never ask us to do something He Himself didn't do.

> *"When you lift up the Son of Man, then you will know that I am He, and that I do nothing of Myself; but as My Father taught Me, I speak these things. And He who sent Me is with Me. The Father has not left Me alone, for I always do those things that please Him." John 8:28-29*

Jesus' model of discipleship will not work if you do not choose to submit to Him wholeheartedly. Submission will be discussed more in a later section of this curriculum.

REFLECTION AND DISCUSSION

What are some components of being on a "team?"

What does it look like to be submitted to a team captain, and to whom is the team captain submitted?

What are some things that you expect from team captains and team coaches?

How did Jesus model submission to the Father?

What examples in the Old Testament point us toward the future of Jesus' model?

LESSON 4 – T.E.A.M.S. THE DISCIPLESHIP MODEL OF JESUS

To quote the life of Jesus shows us how to navigate discipleship correctly. Through His original "team" of disciples, the church was established. However, these disciples were not older, mature Christians. In fact, many sources point to the disciples being young adults or even teenagers, possibly between the ages of 13 and 20![i] The implication here is staggering. These young men and women had the opportunity to start out the right way in their spiritual journey by sitting under the Messiah Himself![ii] Their journeys to spiritual maturity were not easy, and not all of them made it (Judas), but because these disciples replicated what they saw Jesus say and do, the church of God grew, and the Great Commission came to life. Why mess with a perfect method? Let's do it Jesus' way!

Exploring Scripture Exercise:

The Word of God shows us that Jesus' method for discipleship consisted of **teaching, encouraging, advising, modeling, and serving.** Although this curriculum will examine many passages in the Gospel books to detail Jesus' model, take some time before we dive in to see what you know! What stories come to mind of Jesus using these methods of discipleship as He interacted with the disciples, the masses, and individuals during his ministry on earth?

1. **Teach**: Jesus instructs His disciples on how to live a gospel-centered life.

2. **Encourage**: Jesus speaks hope and life into the situations and futures of His disciples.

3. **Advise**: Jesus guides His disciples to take steps to live righteously and be a light to others.

4. **Model**: Jesus demonstrates what it looks like to live holy, selfless, righteous, submitted, and obedient at all times.

5. **Serve**: Jesus consistently respects, honors, and loves God and others through His words and actions.

While some of this seems obvious, the truth is that we don't always do the best job of living out the aspects of this model. We must be intentional in our pursuit to be in discipleship and to be discipled. Sticking to this method is difficult because it requires self-sacrifice and submission to the work of the Spirit. Nonetheless, realizing that discipleship is confined to Jesus' plan and purpose opens our eyes to our own needs, shortcomings, and even hurts, as we have experienced in our relationships with others.

Reflective Exercise:

Which actions in T.E.A.M.S are the most difficult to walk out on as one being discipled? What about those discipling?

Have there been times when you've reacted negatively to one aspect of these methods? If yes, why?

PRACTICAL APPLICATION

Because all of Jesus' teachings are beneficial in all circumstances and for all people, consider some ways you can begin to apply the T.E.A.M.S method of Jesus in your everyday relationships and encounters with people you know and people you don't know.

LESSON 5 – DISCIPLESHIP GONE WRONG

When studying the Gospels and the early church fathers, we should quickly be alerted to any red flags in our current church culture when engaging in discipleship. So, for the sole purpose of providing clarity about discipleship and because so many may have been hurt and wounded by someone in the church in the discipleship process, we must address what discipleship is NOT:

Manipulative - the person discipling is using their position of influence to affect the person being discipled for personal gain.

Controlling - the person discipling is unwilling to be flexible in the process, is self-serving, and is unwilling to admit when wrong.

Degrading - the person doing the discipling leads with insecurities and belittles the person being discipled through words or actions.

Condemning - the person discipling shames the person being discipled for not having the same standards.

Abusive - the person discipling uses their authority to emotionally and physically manipulate the person being discipled for personal gain.

Impatient - the person discipling does most of the talking and listens very little.

Deceptive - the person discipling prioritizes personal preferences more than biblical principles and is easily offended.

A good look at these words and their descriptions shows us that counterfeit discipleship opposes God's heart and His intent in us being transformed into the image of His son. If we aren't imitating Jesus, what and who are we imitating? This is a severe implication that we must consider. Discipleship "gone wrong" can negatively impact our spiritual, mental, and physical health! Some ways this is displayed in our lives can be through anxiety, fear, insecurities, isolation, walking away from Christianity, and, in many cases, idolatry.

Questions for Discussion and Meditation:

The Word of God shows us that Jesus' method for discipleship consisted of **teaching, encouraging, advising, modeling, and serving.** Although this curriculum will examine many passages in the Gospel books to detail Jesus' model, take some time before we dive in to see what you know! What stories come to mind of Jesus using these methods of discipleship as He interacted with the disciples, the masses, and individuals during his ministry on earth?

Have you been in a situation where someone treated you in one of these ways? How did that make you feel?

Are you recognizing that some relationships or leaders in your life have been or are currently operating in one of these dysfunctional ways? How do you feel about this?

PRACTICAL APPLICATION

If you're finding yourself in a situation where you are or have been the recipient of this type of behavior in discipleship, listen carefully:

The Lord loves you; He is sad that this happened to you. He disapproves of this behavior, and He wants to restore you and redeem all that was stolen from you and done to you today.

(Psalm 147:3, John 11:33)

Consider doing the following to receive healing and restoration from unhealthy relationships, such as those we are describing:

1. Professional Counseling
2. Inner Healing
3. Safe Church Community (this will be discussed more in the next unit)

LESSON 6 – LEVELS OF DISCIPLESHIP: AN OVERVIEW

Jesus' ministry model and its continuation by the apostles through the development of the church show that discipleship can organically occur in large and smaller contexts. The T.E.A.M.S model can and should be evident in all three levels of discipleship: the local church, small group community, and mentorship. This curriculum is designed to walk through the T.E.A.M.S model at each level so that discipleship is ongoing and thriving within the body of Christ. No teammate should be left behind.

Level 1: The Local Church

Discipleship at the local church level occurs when individuals submit to a family of God known as a church (a living organism), where every part belongs and finds its health in the right relationship with every other part. According to Ephesians 4:11-16, the Church truly exists to build up the body until all its members grow into maturity, which is the fullness of Christ. Also, only when each member is working together does the body successfully work to build itself up in love.

"Everyone kept feeling a sense of awe...and all those who believed were together and had all things in common."

(Acts 2:43-44)

Considering the T.E.A.M.S model, in what ways can discipleship happen in a local church outside of community groups that contribute to discipling people, even in large numbers?

Level 2: Community

Discipleship in Christian community looks like committing to a smaller group of individuals on a more intimate level that will take participants to a deeply spiritual and personal level of the heart and soul with one another. God created people with an innate desire to connect with Him and one another. Oftentimes, these people will be a source of accountability, a trusted voice of counsel, and your biggest intercessors.

"They were continually devoting themselves to the apostles' teaching, and fellowship, to the breaking of bread and prayer."

(Acts 2:42)

This type of community is different than a group of people you hang out with for fun, although fun should be a part of this type of community. How might this type of community differ from other friend groups or social groups in your life? Take a moment to evaluate if you have this type of community.

Level 3: Mentorship

Paying intentional attention to one's relationship with God is accompanied by the prayerful and discerning presence of someone who guides and is nurturing in the growth and direction of that relationship. Mentorship carries a deeper purpose, and the goal is to shape the mentee's understanding of living and looking like Jesus in word and deed.

"Follow my example, as I follow the example of Christ."

(1 Corinthians 11:1)

Paul mentored several individuals, and many of them accompanied Him in ministry. Have you ever walked with someone this way or considered the need for this kind of relationship? Journal or write below about the possible benefits of this type of relationship and what characteristics a mentor should have.

LESSON 7 – COVENANT IN DISCIPLESHIP

All biblical relationships are inherently based on the concept of covenant, or a mutual agreement to the terms of the relationship. Covenant was part of God's original plan to build a relationship with His beloved human creations. Covenant is about more than just building trust and loyalty; it involves teaching us how to truly love others the way God loves us in every relationship.

Establishing a covenant with each other is not meant to be abusive or legalistic, but to help us live with an eternal kingdom mindset here on earth. There will be no conflict, quarreling, anger, or sin in Heaven. While we will not achieve this perfection in our relationships here on earth, it should be our goal to pursue it.

A Biblical Overview of Covenant

In Exodus 19, God establishes a covenant with the Israelite people, expressing that they will be His chosen people if they obey His commands. The people reply with an affirmative response to the proposed agreement. However, the Israelite people did not prove faithful on their end of the covenant. Deuteronomy 28 details God's gracious renewal of this covenant after the people demonstrated ungratefulness and rebellion during their time in the wilderness.

Much of the Septuagint, or the first five books of the Bible, lays out details of the covenant. The book of Leviticus maps out the extent of the "law," which was to be a guide to help the people pursue holy living and provide protective guardrails to survive in a fallen world. However, as the narrative of the Old Testament develops, it becomes evident that the people of God are just not capable of meeting the standards of the law and that the law, which was designed to aid the people in keeping covenant, was not sufficient in not just keeping the people in bounds, but also covering the sins that cause the breach in covenant. God had a bigger, better, and complete plan ready.

One of the biggest mistakes of spiritual formation is forgetting the God of the Old Testament and the God of the New Testament are the same and His covenantal nature does not change. God visited earth as a man, Jesus, and established a New Covenant through His death, burial, and resurrection. However, Jesus first came to clarify the aspects of the law that people "claimed" to follow, and He did this by establishing an eternal means of discipleship in believers through the indwelling Spirit. This New Covenant still holds the same basic principle:

God is faithful, and we need help to remain faithful. This time, our help comes in an everlasting form through Jesus and His eternal Spirit.

Exploring Scripture Exercise:

Pause and read the following Scriptures. Connect the principles and values of the Old Testament Covenant that are fulfilled and maybe even amplified through Jesus' establishment of a New Covenant and consider how that applies to discipleship.

Deuteronomy 28: 1-34

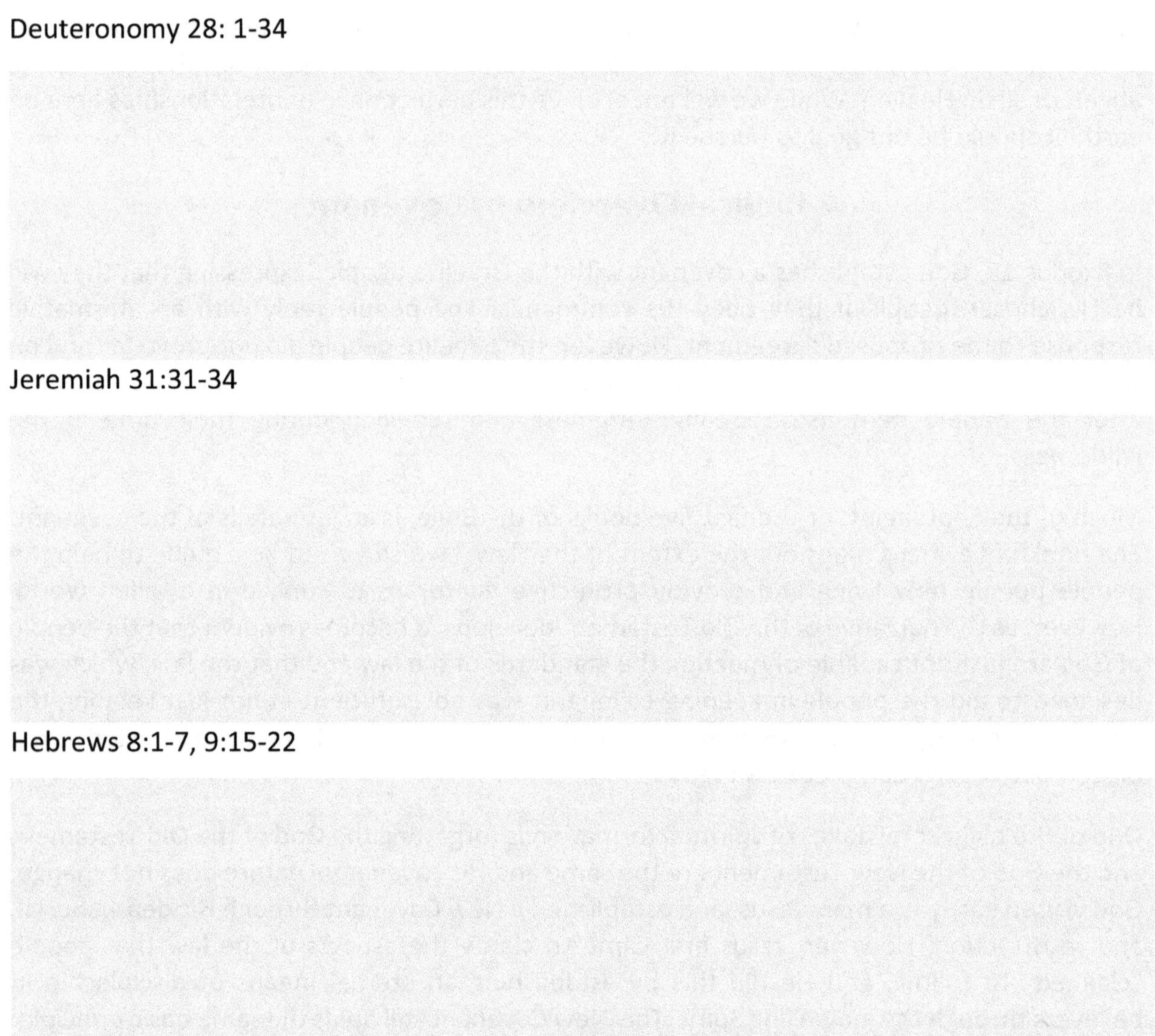

Jeremiah 31:31-34

Hebrews 8:1-7, 9:15-22

Discipleship and the Role of Covenant

How does a Biblical view of covenant influence discipleship? What does it mean to be in covenant with someone in a discipleship relationship, and why is it significant? Remember, all covenants are built on mutually agreed-upon terms. Without a covenant, relationships lack a foundation, transparency, and the ability to produce fruit.

Those involved in discipleship must understand that the terms in this relationship should be based on the *entire* scripture, not just a few verses taken out of context. Therefore, at a minimum, those leading discipleship should be committed to making disciples, modeling the likeness of Jesus, and providing godly edification and encouragement to those under their care. This truly reflects the core message of the Epistles. Paul, Peter, James, Jude, and John write to keep the Church aligned with God's ways and are not afraid to speak truth to do so. Thus, those receiving discipleship at any level should commit to becoming followers of Christ, observing and adopting principles that reflect Jesus in words, thoughts, and actions, and receiving edification and encouragement with a submissive spirit.

The needs above are not exhaustive, and we will cover more components of a healthy mentor-mentee relationship later in this curriculum. Many of these are natural, negotiable terms that depend on individual needs, such as boundaries and expectations. The most important thing is that both parties keep these principles aligned with Scripture and remain committed not to abandon ship when it gets tough. While there may be times when we need to withdraw from certain situations, we must remember that God will guide us and make it clear. God never broke the covenant; man did. We must do our part to model God and not our flesh when we commit to one another and walk through life together.

Reflection and Discussion Activity

Being in a relationship with others is a big commitment. Take a moment to reflect on the relationships in your life. Are you truly committed? Do you often feel tempted to "jump ship" when things get tough? What aspects of covenant relationships mentioned in this section make you uncomfortable or concern you?

Once you identify the answer to these questions, pray and ask God to reveal the "why" or root cause of these issues.

LESSON 8 – PREPARATION FOR DISCIPLESHIP

All Discipleship is a commitment. The truth is that you can't make disciples until you've been discipled. The discipleship process is ongoing. You won't be ready to disciple until you have been discipled. So, what makes someone ready for discipleship? Salvation! Once you say yes to Jesus, you have begun your first discipling relationship. He is our ultimate disciple: how to disciple and be discipled.

Once we say yes to Jesus, He calls us into community with other believers, both for discipling and being discipled. All Christians are called to examine the condition of the heart before entering any discipleship to ensure that the relationship is safe, healthy, Christ-like, and Christ-exalting. As we just learned, "discipleship-gone-wrong" can be traumatizing and damaging. Preparing yourself in the following ways can ensure that your heart and mind are ready to receive what Christ has for you.

1.CULTIVATE HUMILITY

See Matthew 11:29, Philippians 2:3-4, Colossians 3:12

As our perfect discipleship model, Jesus gives us the blueprint for where to begin! Jesus' character is self-described as gentle and humble, often choosing to operate from a servant's heart.

In what ways can we cultivate a Christ-like humility?

How is that humility different than the world's definition of humility?

When we operate with a heart of humility, our posture brings us into a submissive partnership with the Lord and creates a teachable heart.

Submitted Partnership

See Romans 12:10 and Hebrews 10:25

You must partner with the Lord and those He brings to disciple you. Jesus modeled this for us as He walked in constant obedience to the Father in His earthly ministry.

What does a submitted partnership in discipleship look like? Must we be submitted to humans or only to Jesus?

Teachability

See 1 Peter 5:5, Proverbs 4:5, Acts 8:31

All discipling involves teaching, but it is a choice to hear and receive. Are you willing to be teachable and receive from others?

Ask the Lord to reveal anything prohibiting you from being teachable, whether it is pride, fear, anxiety, etc. What could be the root cause of these issues, and what steps can you take to overcome them before entering discipleship?

When we cultivate humility, we mirror Christ's character and prepare our hearts to be led by the people He gifted us in discipleship. Let us close this section by reflecting on what stands in the way of us willingly choosing His identity of humility. Journal any roadblocks that come to mind and ask the Lord to begin knocking them down.

2.CULTIVATE EAGERNESS

See Luke 14:27, Mark 16:15, 1 Corinthians 9:24

God calls us all to be disciples and qualifies us all through Christ. He gifts us explicitly, uniquely, and individually according to His Spirit with talents, skills, and assignments to further the kingdom of God. This should drive us, like a runner desperate to cross her finish line!

What parts of your walk with God excite you? What ways of serving Him make you feel fulfilled?

What makes you eager to know Him more?

When we cultivate an eagerness to fulfill our God-given purpose, God meets us where we are to teach us patience, help us put on His identity, and fuel us with His vision for us!

Patience

See Galatians 5:22-23

The process of discipleship takes time because it involves the continual work of the Spirit. Kevin Vanhoozer, a theologian and writer on discipleship practices, describes discipleship as a process during which we are "active." [i] Authentic discipleship requires a lot of intentionality and commitment to see the fruit of spiritual maturity. The disciples walked with Jesus for the entirety of Jesus' ministry on earth, yet some did not see the fruit of that until after His resurrection and ascension into heaven.

How should you adjust your expectations regarding time and heart commitment to grow in this area to prepare you as you enter discipleship with others?

Identity

See 2 Corinthians 5:17, 1 Peter 2:19, 1 John 1:12, and 3:1-2

You are a child of God. You are raised with Christ, a new creation. Therefore, you should want to exemplify that to the world and your relationships with others.

Do you fully grasp what it means to be a child of God? If not, are you ready to be discipled in this foundational truth that you were raised with Christ to walk in righteousness and are no longer a slave to sin?

Do you desire to be a safe person who offers the love, grace, shelter, and presence of Jesus, who exudes this identity? How can you demonstrate to others that you desire to be a safe yet confident person for others?

Vision

See 1 Corinthians 12, Acts 20:24

God calls us all to be disciples; He qualifies us all through Christ, yet He gifts us explicitly, uniquely, and individually according to His Spirit with talents, skills, and assignments to further the kingdom of God.

Do you know how God has equipped you?

Can you identify who you want to become in the discipleship process and how you must be equipped to walk out your God-appointed assignments here on earth?

When we cultivate eagerness in discipleship, we grow in patience, take on our God-given identity, and see with His perfect vision how to accomplish all He sets before us. Let us close this section by reflecting on the impact of discipleship progression on your sense of self and belonging in Christ's body. Journal any fears or hesitations to this calling and submit them before the Lord.

Discernment

As God develops us through our eagerness in discipleship, he maintains us through wisdom and discernment, which helps us to be conformed into His image by being aware of that which is and is not of His image (1 John 4:1, Philippians 1:9-10 and Romans 12:2). Discernment is developed through many of the spiritual disciplines that are encouraged and activated through discipleship, such as a prayer, Bible study and meditation and Christian community.

Think of a time when you've had a "feeling" or a "knowing" that something was of God or not of God and reflect on the indicators that this was discernment from God?

Likewise, recall a time when you've acted or spoken without discernment or witnessed someone else doing the same? What was the outcome of these moments? How did God correct, redeem or even restore those moments from a lapse of discernment? Reflect on any growth that came from those mistakes.

Reflective Exercise:

Before going any further in this curriculum, be encouraged to spend some time open-handed with the Lord. Ask Him to examine your heart and reveal any areas mentioned above that you need to allow Him to address or other areas of your life that need to be healed or addressed before committing to discipleship. "While perfection is not expected, it's wise to ask the Lord to reveal and deal with anything in you that could hinder the discipleship process or your relationship with your brothers and sisters in Christ. As the process begins, discipleship—led by the Holy Spirit—should naturally begin to address these areas."

If you can't find the words, try using this prayer:

Lord God, I desire to be more like You, and I know that discipleship is a part of this journey. Please show me what in my heart needs to be addressed before I go any further so that I can enter into discipleship with a pure heart, ready to walk with others as Christ did. I surrender my will and pride in this moment and commit to doing all you instruct me to do as I take this step

PART 2:
PLANTING THE SEEDS

Examining Jesus' Model of Discipleship through the T.E.A.M.S. method

INTRODUCTION

INTRODUCTION

As we learned in the previous section, Jesus, the Son of God, was the initiator and author of discipleship. Discovering who Jesus is, is the catalyst for and foundation of, discipleship. He also mandated us to go and make disciples, so there must be a way for the Christian community to do this well. A method of discipleship that uses the model established by Jesus during his earthly ministry, as evidenced in the Gospels, can solve this problem. Through the teaching, encouraging, advising, modelling, and serving of Jesus, this model successfully equipped and positioned the disciples to enact the Great Commission and establish the church.

In this section of Cultivate, we will explore the life of Jesus as documented by the authors of the Gospels to establish how Jesus used each of these methods to disciple not just the "twelve" or the "seventy-two" but the masses and learn how to apply these today.

LESSON 9 – TEACH

When we hear the word "teach," our minds immediately go to a school classroom with books, computers, notebooks, and recorders. While that is one form of intentional education, opportunities for instruction are available to us 24/7 through multiple avenues such as books, television, social media, billboards, and museums, to name a few. However, just merely being in the presence of the man Jesus meant constant availability for instruction for anyone around Him.

In the New Testament, the word, διδάσκω, or didaskō, is most used to describe the "teaching" role as we know it in our culture. This word means: to hold discourse (communicate orally) to instruct, impart instruction, or instill doctrine.

In Jewish cultures, teachers were called "Rabbis." Rabbis were not just thoroughly educated and instructed themselves but completely immersed and knowledgeable in all Jewish cultural and religious aspects. They were considered the experts on all matters. To be called this was an important distinction that pointed directly to the reputation as being highly educated, honorable, and full of integrity. Jesus was referred to as "Rabbi" on multiple occasions, not just by His disciples but also by those He met through ministry and even by the Pharisees.

Jesus often refers to Himself as "Teacher" (John 13:13, Matthew 23:10, 26:18, etc.). He was a gifted orator, and people gathered around Him to hear Him teach in amazement. Although Jesus taught thousands, often in one sitting, His most intimate teaching occurred during His ministry as He trained up the "twelve" in discipleship. They received instruction from Him that was intentional and specific to their role in building the church through the Great Commission. As Jesus taught others, He used various teaching tactics that we are familiar with, such as the Socratic method (a Greek rhetorical method of instruction widely known and used in Jewish education), storytelling through parables, crafting or quoting wise sayings, and personalized communication.

Exploring Scripture Exercise:

Below are examples of Jesus' teachings given to the twelve disciples who walked with Him. Because Jesus often clarifies doctrine and theology regarding the kingdom living, check your doctrinal knowledge and learn from each other. In the passages below, explore how these teaching moments:

- express the character of God and the deity of Jesus
- demonstrate the love of God and the extent to which we are to love God and love others
- clarify the Law and prophecy by showing what true love of God and obedience look like
- certify the reality, the truth, and the power of the Gospel message.

Matthew 10 – Jesus' instructions for sending out the disciples.

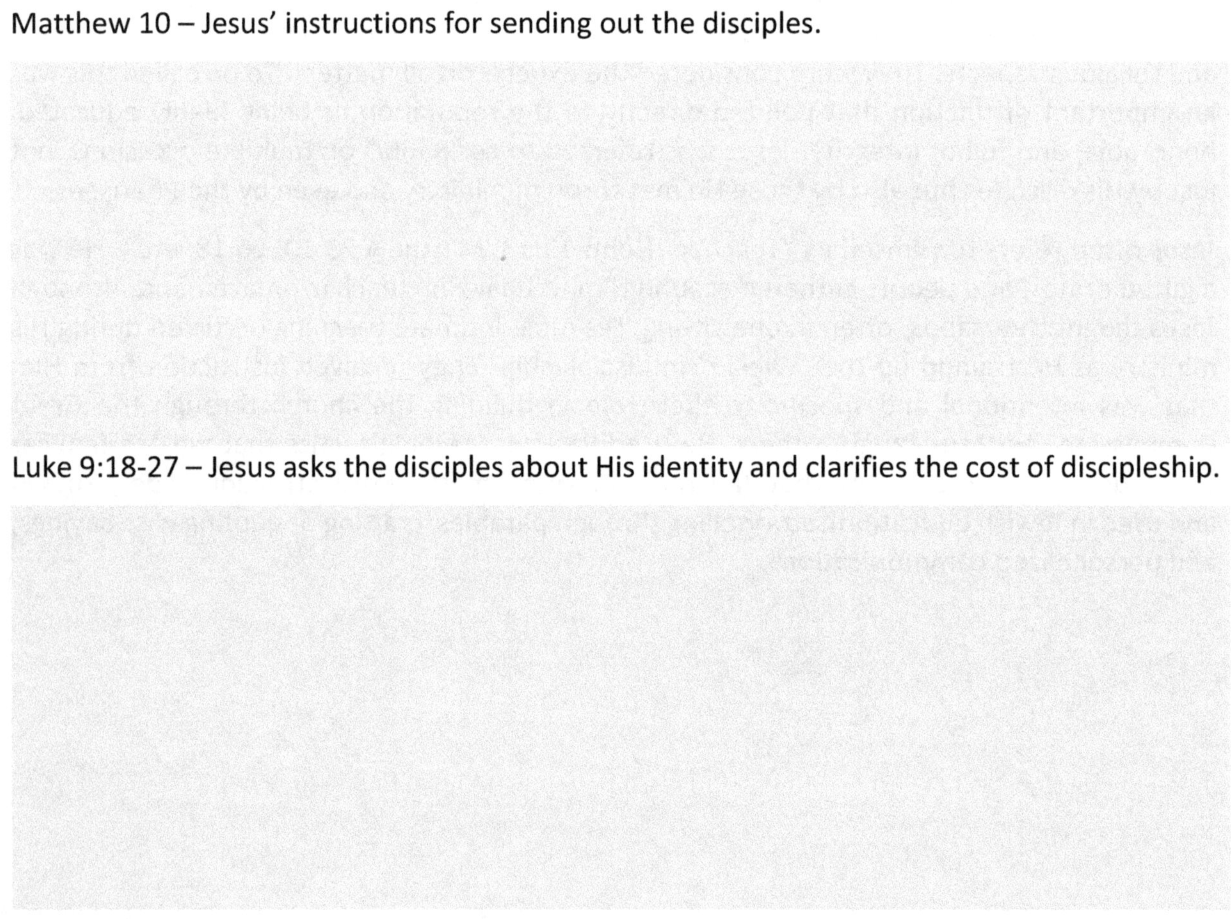

Luke 9:18-27 – Jesus asks the disciples about His identity and clarifies the cost of discipleship.

Lesson 9 | Teach

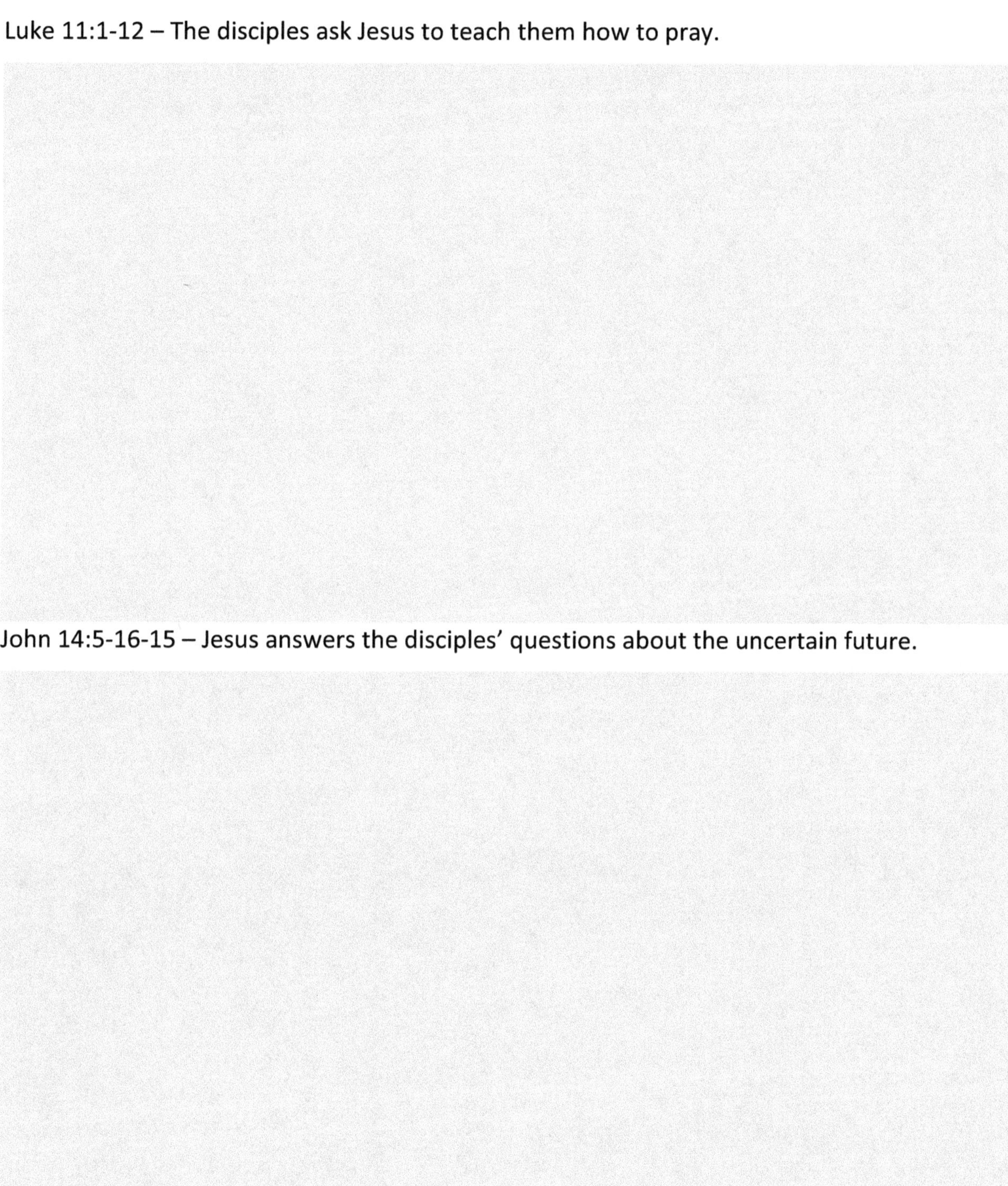

Luke 11:1-12 – The disciples ask Jesus to teach them how to pray.

John 14:5-16-15 – Jesus answers the disciples' questions about the uncertain future.

LESSON 10 – ENCOURAGEMENT

When we Encouragement plays a vital role in healthy, godly discipleship. Where the other letters in the T.E.A.M.S model primarily call us toward a goal, encouragement refreshes us where we are and gives us a renewed purpose and perspective. If we follow the sports analogy, times of encouragement can be viewed as timeouts or pep talks that highlight our successes and give us a second wind to keep pushing toward our team goal.

However, as those who have played on a team know, not all encouragement is equal. Words meant to be encouraging can often be too "fluffy" to be meaningful, too vague to be helpful, or too pacifying to inspire change. From the life and ministry of Jesus, we see that godly encouragement has the following characteristics:

1.Godly encouragement is realistic.

Before offering His disciples words of hope and life, Jesus often addressed the reality of living in a fallen world as fallible, imperfect people. While He never dipped into hopelessness or pessimism, Jesus did not shy away from the fact that a life lived in submission to God would have periods of stretching, changing, lack, or difficulty (John 16:33, Matthew 6:25-34, Matthew 7:24-27, Luke 12:4-5).

2.Godly encouragement is directional.

Where unhelpful encouragement can leave a person stagnant, godly encouragement calls them to a higher, better standard. Jesus did not point out the disciples' struggles to brow-beat or embarrass them. Nor did He gloss over the areas of their lives that did not meet God's standard of holiness. Instead, He spoke about life and truth from a place of love in these areas.

Jesus encouraged His disciples to make small, attainable steps towards righteousness. When His disciples asked Him to increase their faith, Jesus responded that faith as small as a mustard seed would be honored. When He called them to give to those in need, adopt a life of prayer, and fast, He encouraged them with the promise that God would see their obedience (Matthew 6). In that same chapter, He called them to put aside their anxieties, not because life would be perfect, but because they were loved and seen by the Provider of all that they would need.

3.Godly encouragement is hopeful.

Jesus's encouragement was filled with hope for a deep joy, an inexplicable peace, and an abiding love that would be theirs despite the world around them. It called them to draw close to their Father in the present and look forward to a future with Him, where the cares of this world would be no more. Jesus's encouragement was eternal and built on a firm foundation.

Exploring Scripture and Critical Thinking Exercise

Use the passages below and note what Jesus acknowledged about the disciples' current reality, and what He promised in response:

John 16:33

Future Hope

Current Reality

Lesson 10 | Encouragement

Matthew 7:24-25

Future Hope

Current Reality

Matthew 6:25-30

Future Hope

Current Reality

Lesson 10 | Encouragement

Luke 12:6-7

Future Hope

Current Reality

LESSON 11 – ADVISE

"For unto us a child has been born for us; a son has been given to us. And the dominion will be on His shoulder, and His name is called Wonderful Counselor [yāʿas], Mighty God, Everlasting Father, Prince of Peace."

(Isaiah 9:6, LEB)

This is the most well-known prophecy declared about Jesus before His birth, sung and read by many during Christmas. The word "counselor" means to advise and give counsel. So, the Hebrew can help us understand that Jesus' eternal ministry would be marked by His extraordinary advice and impeccable discernment.

Let's be honest about this topic for a minute. We can recall times when we've sought counsel and received one of the three types of advice: bad, sound, or godly. Can you differentiate?

A Moment for Discussion

Stop and differentiate between the three types of advice mentioned above.

Bad advice takes you outside the will of God and contradicts scripture. Good advice makes sense logically, according to man's ideas. Godly advice comes directly from the heart of the Father, keeps you in the will of God at all costs, and glorifies God in the process. Good advice can be godly advice, but sometimes good advice is just a good "man-made" idea, but not God's best for you.

In addition, we can all recall moments where we've received advice through our asking and received "unsolicited" advice. Did you know that true discipleship leaves room for solicited and unsolicited advice and that Jesus models having the discernment to handle it perfectly according to the Father's purposes?

Discuss times when you've experienced all three types of advice, whether solicited or unsolicited, and how you successfully navigated or possibly learned from those moments.

Jesus' advice was always godly because He is God. As we look at Jesus' model for offering advice, we can learn as much about being postured to receive advice as we can about giving it. When giving advice, Jesus discerned the approach and timing that would display the Father's heart and be the most edifying for the receiver.

Jesus Giving Solicited Advice

In Matthew 19:16-22, Jesus is approached by the rich, young ruler with a question about how to obtain eternal life.

Exploring Scripture Exercise:

Read the passage above together and answer the following questions:

1. What is the nature of Jesus' relationship with this person?

2. What approach does Jesus take in advising Him on how to gain eternal life? (Note what Jesus did and did not do during this interaction.)

3. What was the man's response to Jesus' advice?

Jesus Giving Unsolicited Advice

Jesus discipled and commissioned more than just those twelve men who walked intimately with Him. Luke 10 documents Jesus sending an additional 72 men out to preach, heal, and operate in power and authority to advance the Kingdom of God. He filled them with wisdom and advice on operating in the field as He sent them. After following His advice, they came back excited about all they had witnessed and done in the name of Jesus. However, Jesus uses that moment to offer some unexpected and unsolicited advice that would be invaluable to them as they continue their ministry.

Exploring Scripture Exercise:

Read Luke 10:17-20 and answer the following questions:

1. What is the nature of Jesus' relationship with the seventy-two men?

2. Why do you think Jesus found it appropriate to interrupt this time of rejoicing to offer unsolicited advice?

3. Although we are not told the response of the seventy-two after receiving this advice, what does each response, both acceptance of and rejection of the advice, reveal about the hearts of the recipients?

Personal Reflection

Discipleship is serious business. Receiving advice from someone and giving advice to someone requires a significant amount of trust. That trust is built through investing in relationships with those you are to walk with in discipleship. Although there should be fruit available for you to judge that will indicate the validity of the advice, testing the advice we receive is still essential. What are some ways that you can test the advice you receive before accepting or dismissing it? Are you genuinely open to receiving and accepting advice as a form of discipleship, especially advice that might be the opposite of what you would prefer to hear? Think of a time that you received good advice, but it was a "hard pill to swallow." Or consider a time that you gave advice, and it was rejected. What happened to your heart in those moments? Evaluate your response and consider how knowing what you do now can impact this aspect of discipleship moving forward.

LESSON 12 – MODEL

Modeling is a developmental process that naturally occurs throughout human life, involving imitation through observation. Babies and toddlers depend on their parents' words and actions to learn basic skills, and as they grow, they continue to imitate behaviors, speech, and mannerisms from their parents. Adults also experience modeling in various forms within their relationships and communities.

In some way or another, we are all frequently modeling to each other, which is a sobering reality. This means there is ***intentional*** and ***casual modeling***, just as there is ***intentional*** and ***casual observation***. Both create impressions that are often imitated, sometimes intentionally (consciously), and sometimes unintentionally (subconsciously). Jesus' modeling in discipleship was always intentional, even if those He discipled were observing casually or intentionally.

Consider how modeling works in everyday relationships between spouses, parents and children, friend groups, dating relationships, and workplace colleagues. The more you are around a person, the more you start to talk like them, dress like them, like the same things as them, have the same physical mannerisms as them, etc.

God created us to be impressionable, intending for us to imitate Christ so that we might conform to the image of Christ and be holy image bearers. Good parenting should consist of intentional modeling and an awareness of personal behavior. Jesus, God Himself in human form, was the perfect model for Christian living. Jesus' words, actions, mannerisms, decisions, responses, thoughts, and motives were God-honoring and Spirit-led. The disciples, merely being in His presence, had the opportunity to observe perfection and learn to replicate it through casual and intentional observation. Even when they weren't purposely watching to gain knowledge, like sitting at a table and eating, their casual observation of Jesus' perfect behavior enabled them to replicate it.

Exploring Scripture and Critical Thinking Exercise

Find these moments in Scripture where Jesus modeled something specific to the disciples and discuss the questions below:

Jesus modeling how to handle healing/ministry: Luke 5:38-41

Jesus modeling how to surrender emotions: Matthew 21:12-13, Luke 22:39-45

Jesus modeling how to handle compassion: John 1:43-50

Jesus modeling how to handle conflict: Luke 10:46-50

Jesus modeling how to handle discipline: Luke 10:53-56

Jesus modeling how to handle resistance: Mark 12:13-17

Jesus modeling how to handle persecution: John 18-19, Luke 23:32-34

1. In this instance, were the disciples engaged in intentional or casual observation through Jesus' modeling?

2. What behavior was Jesus modeling here, and were there any specific modeling methods that He used that are familiar to you from everyday life?

3. Was there immediate fruit or response from the modeling, or can you note something in Scripture that indicates fruit from these disciples who have attempted to imitate Jesus' model?

Personal Reflection:

Modeling is the most productive, yet possibly the most destructive method of discipleship. Discuss this reality from the perspective of the one discipling and the one being discipled. How does this reality that modeling is intentional and casual add a sobriety to the discipleship process and even impact your relationships within your various communities?

LESSON 13 – SERVE

"Even the Son of Man came not to be served but to serve, and to give His life as a ransom for many." (Mark 10:45, ESV)

Jesus served His Father.

Jesus' life was marked first and foremost by service to His Father. He testified in John 6:38 that He had come "not to do my own will, but the will of Him who sent me." In verse 40, we see that this will of God has eternal importance for us: "For this is the will of my Father, that everyone who looks on the Son and believes in Him should have eternal life, and I will raise Him up on the last day." (John 6:40, ESV)

Serving God would come at a great cost to Jesus. He would be emptied, humbled, subjected to human frailty, and sacrificed for the people who had rejected Him (Philippians 2). Jesus did not serve because it was easy. He served because He loved the Father who had sent Him and the people He was sent to save.

Jesus served the crowds.

As Jesus lived in service and submission to His Father, His heart was moved with compassion for all He encountered. Out of this compassion, He performed miracles of provision and healing that showed His power and love for all He met (Mark 1:41-42, Mark 8:2, John 11:33).

Jesus served His disciples.

Jesus' love and compassion extended especially toward those closest to His heart. He met His disciples' physical needs throughout their time together and performed a final grand act of service during their last supper. In John 13 and Luke 22, we see Jesus washing His disciples' feet. Knowing all that would happen next, He humbly and lovingly served His friends by washing away the day's dirt, foreshadowing His sacrifice that would spiritually wash them clean mere hours later.

He humbly washed their feet in contrast to their ironic bickering about who would be the greatest (Luke 22). He served them all, including Judas, who would betray Him, and Peter, who would deny Him. In a beautiful full-circle moment, the risen Jesus would serve His disciples another meal. Over a breakfast of fish and bread prepared by Jesus, He would offer Peter a restored relationship with Him, and Peter would redeclare His love for the Savior.

Jesus serves today

Even now, the glorified Jesus is serving His Bride. Hebrews 13:6 reminds us that we can confidently say, "The Lord is my helper; I will not fear. What can man do to me?" He is our great high priest and advocate (Hebrews 10, 1 John 2). Jesus' service was costly, but He has been exalted because of it. Because His heart is for you and me, we reap the benefits of His service for eternity.

Personal Reflective Exercise:

Use the question below to reflect on how this area of discipleship is displayed or needs to be addressed in your life.

1. What is the significance of Jesus primarily serving His Father?

2.What difference does it make to serve from a place of compassion?

3. What is the purpose of serving?

4. What does it look like for you to serve as one being discipled or as the one discipling others?

THE T.E.A.M.S MODEL AND THE EARLY CHURCH

The continuation of Jesus's method of discipleship is evidenced not just in the Book of Acts as the Church is being established through the Great Commission, but also in the Epistles with already established churches. This shows that discipleship is a continual process a believer must submit to during earthly life. In the book of Acts, the disciples had a universal mission to claim and testify to the Lordship of Christ. Part of how they did this was by demonstrating personal conformity to Jesus's lifestyle, which they had witnessed.

Exploring Scripture Exercise:

The first incident of the replication of this model after Jesus's ascension and the coming of the Holy Spirit is Peter's address to the crowds in Acts 2:14-41. In this address alone, the model of Jesus is seen in complete form. Read this section of Scripture together and use the following progression as a guide, stopping to discuss how each of these methods likely impacted those listening.

1. Peter teaches by explaining the meaning of Old Testament scripture and its relevance to Christ (vs.25-28)

2. He encourages by telling them that the promise of salvation is available for all who will heed (vs 39)

3.He advises by telling them they must repent (vs.38)

4.He models by standing up boldly and pleading with them to hear the truth he is sharing (vs. 40)

5.He serves them by baptizing them (vs. 41)

Sometimes the apostles were going with a mission in discipleship sole to encourage a church. Acts 11:22-23 documents Barnabas being sent to encourage the church in Antioch. Other times, discipleship looks like advising, like in Acts 15 when the council got together to figure out how to advise the Gentiles about eating food polluted by idols and other lifestyle issues associated with Christian living. Paul modeled constantly in the face of opposition as a form of discipleship. When Agabus told him he would be bound in Jerusalem in chapter 21, rather than be depressed and defeated, Paul modeled surrender by going anyway and being ok with what was coming for him despite the tears and pleading of his disciples and friends. Serving through ministry is actively seen throughout the book of Acts, as the apostles go out and heal and deliver many under the power of the Holy Spirit (Acts 5:12-16).

Seeing Jesus' model continued in the development of the Church in this way should be a clarion call for the modern Church to do the same, as Jesus has not returned. All of the Saints, regardless of age or maturity in the faith, should continually be discipled until that time.

Questions for Discussion:

1. How has exploring Jesus' model of discipleship clarified what discipleship is and what it is supposed to look like?

2. What misperceptions have you had about discipleship that have been clarified through this study so far?

3. What are some action steps that you feel the Lord is prompting you to take to begin to practically see discipleship be present and intentional in your life?

PART 3:

Reaping the Harvest in the Biggest Field

Cultivation of Discipleship in the Local Church

LESSON 14 – DISCIPLESHIP AND THE CHURCH

Jesus is the first person to use the word *church* or ἐκκλησία. This word is a Greek compound word, with its components ek, meaning "out from and to," and *kaléō*, which means "to call." We can see discipleship's foundational implications in the local church's formation, growth, and stability! Exploring church history shows how discipleship is intermingled into all aspects of our gatherings when we come together.

Cultivating and embracing discipleship benefits the local church by:

Creating unity through community.

(Acts 2:42-47)

Providing edification through teaching and admonishment.

(Colossians 3:16-17)

Serving one another by providing physical and spiritual means of support. (Philippians 2:3 and 1 Peter 4:9-10)

Empowering and equipping the community members to use their gifts for

the Kingdom of God.

(1 Corinthians 12:12-31)

Establish leadership to oversee the spiritual growth and facilitate the

protection of the church community.

(Ephesians 4:11-13)

Loving and giving honor to one another. (Romans 12:16)

Co-laboring with one another to evangelize and spread the Gospel's good news. (Philippians 1:3-8)

This part of this curriculum will evaluate how our corporate unit and its gatherings can successfully navigate discipleship to see how the fruits of these benefits impact the maturity of the individuals in our churches.

Questions for Discussion

1. Look at the breakdown of the Greek word ἐκκλησία. How might there be insight in the words "ek" and "kaleo" that can connect the foundational nature of discipleship being a component, if not a primary purpose, of the church?

2. Reading the scriptures connected with the benefits above. Think about components and programs within the modern church that are cultivating these benefits. Which benefits are the least often seen executed well in the local church, and why?

3. What practical ways do you see the benefits being executed in the local church you attend?

LESSON 15 – JESUS, DISCIPLESHIP AND THE CHURCH

The book of Acts shares the history and development of the church of Jesus Christ. However, the Gospels reveal that during his 33-year earthly ministry, Jesus put everything in place to expand His kingdom on earth successfully. Jesus paved the way for establishing and growing His church through discipleship. In two specific instances, Jesus uses the word "church" in His interactions with His disciples. What can we learn about the purposes of the church from these two passages?

> *"And I tell you that you are Peter, and on this rock I will build my church, and the gates of Hades will not overcome it. I will give you the keys of the kingdom of heaven; whatever you bind on earth will be bound in heaven, and whatever you loose on earth will be loosed in heaven."*

Then He ordered His disciples not to tell anyone He was the Messiah. (See Matthew 16:13-20 for the entire context.)

> *"If your brother or sister sins, point out their fault, just between the two of you. If they listen to you, you have won them over. But if they will not listen, take one or two others along so that 'every matter may be established by the testimony of two or three witnesses. If they still refuse to listen, tell it to the church; and if they refuse to listen even to the church, treat them as you would a pagan or a tax collector. Truly I tell you, whatever you bind on earth will be bound in heaven, and whatever you loose on earth will be loosed in heaven. Again, truly I tell you that if two of you on earth agree about anything they ask for, it will be done for them by my Father in heaven. For where two or three gather in my name, there am I with them."* (Matt. 18 for the entire context.)

Jesus designed the Church, comprised of His beloved followers, to move in His delegated authority and power in unity here on earth, to be vessels of the Gospel and to protect its testimony.

Critical Thinking Exercise

From these scriptures, how can we see that Jesus had planned for His disciples to do the legwork, as all His teaching and "discipling" laid the groundwork? Also, how might we see a foreshadowing of how the assembly of people plays a vital role in discipling each other?

LESSON 16 - DISCIPLESHIP AND THE ESTABLISHMENT OF THE CHURCH

Consider the following timeline of important events and mark the role of the disciples and the use of discipleship through the important events:

Jesus gathers His disciples -- Jesus calls Peter "the rock -- Jesus teaches on the role of the church -- Jesus dies and rises again -- Jesus shares the "Great Commission" with His disciples -- Jesus ascends foretelling of the coming of the Spirit -- Pentecost -- Peter and the other apostles are empowered to preach the gospel -- Peter has vision and begins to preach to Gentiles -- Saul encounters Jesus and is commissioned -- Paul begins to preach the Gospel to the Gentiles.

The complete list of established churches is likely too great to count. Although Paul is the central figure of the New Testament, we know that John, James, and Peter were addressing churches or at least a collective of Christians with whom they were in a relationship for a specific apostolic purpose. Their purposes for writing were all centered around protecting the integrity of the Gospel message and spreading the news of the risen Lord Jesus, who brought salvation to all peoples. The content of their letters contains elements of teaching, encouragement, advice, modeling, and service. Sound familiar?

Although Jesus created and established the church during His reign on earth, the idea of like-minded believers in discipleship-like relationships is not an original New Testament concept. The Israelites had various leaders, prophets, judges, kings, and counsels to whom they were held accountable. Their "tribes" often worked together, bought land together, ate meals together, worshipped together, and intermarried together (yikes!!).

A good look at the Old Testament shows us that maintaining relationships with like-minded people has a twofold purpose that carries into Jesus' purposes for the church mentioned in the previous section: to protect God's people and to empower God's people to carry out His purposes.

Exploratory Scripture Exercise

Here are some common characteristics of the "church" in the New Testament and the "Israelite community" in the Old Testament that are evident in scripture. Take the following list and find examples of the New and Old Testaments and discuss any directives in Scripture that explain the "why" behind these characteristics.

1. They were a group of individuals with commonalities in the faith.

2. The people in their community "did life" together by eating, worshipping, sharing land and possessions, etc.

3. The group had some form of leadership to which they were held accountable.

4. There were specific gatherings where they met to worship, praise, use gifts, and hear an exhortation.

LESSON 17 - CHURCH LEADERSHIP AND DISCIPLESHIP

God does not leave His people abandoned in the spiritual or the natural! While He is always present and the ultimate authority in our lives, He is a good Father who raises leaders within our corporate gatherings to guide and protect His flock through discipleship. However, even those leaders need co-laborers because it takes a village. Various denominations have different forms of leadership established because it is a Biblical precedent. A hard look at scripture shows us that Godly leadership's ultimate purpose is to disciple. However, a solid leadership system with co-laborers can help carry the mantle of leadership to avoid chaos and share in the responsibility of shepherding the flock.

Within the Exodus story, we see the first Biblical leadership challenge addressed and solved. God divinely called Moses to lead the Israelites out of Egypt, into the wilderness, through the wilderness, and to the promised land. However, quickly into that journey, Moses discovered that God's collective people are problematic and high maintenance. The Israelite people were easily inconvenienced, rattled, disgruntled, and ungrateful, constantly needing supervision and shepherding. When Moses's father-in-law saw the stress and burden that Moses was carrying, He advised Moses to appoint leaders to help Him judge the needs of the people. In both the Exodus account (Exodus 18) and the Deuteronomy account (Deuteronomy 1), these men are referred to as judges or officers. The number of these men was said to be in the thousands. However, even that was not sufficient. Moses needed a core group of people, anointed and set apart by the Lord, to help Him.

> *Moses heard the people of every family wailing at the entrance to their tents. The Lord became exceedingly angry, and Moses was troubled. He asked the Lord, "Why have you brought this trouble on your servant? What have I done to displease you that you put the burden of all these people on me? Did I conceive all these people? Did I give them birth? Why do you tell me to carry them in my arms, as a nurse carries an infant, to the land you promised on oath to their ancestors? Where can I get meat for all these people? They keep wailing to me, 'Give us meat to eat!' I cannot carry all these people by myself; the burden is too heavy for me. If this is how you are going to treat me, please go ahead and kill me—if I have found favor in your eyes—and do not let me face my own ruin." Lord said to Moses: "Bring me seventy of Israel's elders who are*

> *known to you as leaders and officials among the people. Have them come to the tent of meeting, that they may stand there with you. I will come down and speak with you there, and I will take some of the power of the Spirit that is on you and put it on them. They will share the burden of the people with you so that you will not have to carry it alone."* (Numbers 11:16-20))

The Hebrew word describing these 70 men is translated as elder. What exactly did these men do? They shared many of Moses's tasks, such as settling disputes, directing, correcting behavior, and instructing them on the law. Most importantly, God says that He put the power of the Spirit on them to help share the burden of leading these people. Sounds kind of like discipleship.

Even though God is our ultimate spiritual authority, He put into motion earthly authority during creation.

> *Then God said, "Let us make humanity in our image, in our likeness, so that they may rule over the fish in the sea and the birds in the sky, over the livestock and all the wild animals, and over all the creatures that move along the ground. So God created humanity in His own image, in the image of God He created them, male and female, He created them. God blessed them and said to them, "Be fruitful and increase in number; fill the earth and subdue it. Rule over the fish in the sea and the birds in the sky and over every living creature that moves on the ground.* (Genesis 1:26-28)

God ordains all human authority on earth as a means of order through selfless service. To be a church leader is to be a servant among the people of God. This does not negate His ultimate authority but instead supports His ultimate authority by gifting humankind with a vessel through which His authority flows, an act of service and love to His creation.

> *"Everyone must submit Himself to the governing authorities, for there is no authority except that which God has established. The authorities that exist have been established by God."* (Romans 13:1)

The New Testament church, which is to be our model, was also established with various forms of leadership tasked to use Jesus' model of discipleship to "build up the church." In Ephesians, Paul says that Christ gave the church this leadership to "equip the people for works of service." Yet, we see that various denominations have structures of leadership that differ from one another. Regardless of a church's leadership structure, what matters most is that those leading are leading in the character of Christ, as that is the means through which true discipleship flows. Scripture clearly explains that discipleship occurs through the submission of church leadership as they fulfill their mandates to equip and serve the saints. Remember, a call to leadership is a call to service, not promotion or platform.

Critical Thinking Exercise

Because various churches have differing leadership structures, take a moment to discuss the various forms of leadership modeled for you in your church or churches that you know. How do these models fulfill the purposes of leadership as established by Scripture? Here are some scriptures that can guide your discussion on the various structural elements of church leadership.

Elders: 1 Timothy 3:8-13; 1 Peter 5:1-4

Deacons: 1 Timothy 5:17

LESSON 18 - DISCIPLESHIP GONE WRONG

Addressing Church Hurt and Spiritual Abuse

While appointing specific individuals to church leadership is meant to serve the spiritual health and growth of the members, it's important to acknowledge that many reading this may feel uncomfortable—because the kind of discipleship we're describing can stir up negative emotions tied to past experiences with church leadership. So, the curriculum at this point must pause and sit on the realities of church hurt and spiritual abuse. Any way you look at it, church hurt and spiritual abuse are a result of discipleship gone wrong. There are entire ministries devoted to exposing and ministering to those who have been victims of church hurt and abuse. Because these often occur under the guise of discipleship, this curriculum must join the conversation by providing a guide to help steer discipleship toward Jesus and away from potential hurt and abuse. We want to support the local church, offer hope to the local church, and not deter anyone from the local church. To do that, we must face the triggers and provide those engaged in the curriculum with the tools to identify, discern, and heal so they can still thrive in discipleship in the corporate church setting.

This section may triggering for many of you. Please take a deep breath and know that the best way to combat a trigger and get past it is to face it and be ministered to through the Spirit of the Lord, His Word, and the sisters in Christ with whom you are hopefully going through this curriculum.

Let us simplify by referring to part one: **manipulative, controlling, degrading, condemning, abusive, impatient, or deceptive behavior from a leader or collective group of individuals that leads to a victim's loss of identity or wounds their relationship with Christ, is church hurt and abuse.**

Church hurt and abuse take the Jesus-established, God-honoring, people-serving characteristics of discipleship and pervert them into self-gratifying, self-exalting, self-serving characteristics that not only taint the testimony of Jesus but misrepresent the heart of the Father and wound the body of Christ.

Discipline is a godly aspect of discipleship. Discipline might hurt our feelings, but abuse hurts our identity and our soul. Godly discipline is never manipulative. It might be hard and heavy, but our identity as a child of God is strengthened in discipline, whereas in abuse, it is threatened. In discipline, the person doing the discipling has nothing to gain. In abuse, the person has everything to gain. We have a choice to receive discipline, whereas abuse is forced upon us. This is just one example. Discipline is designed to make us better and protect us, whereas abuse is designed to destroy our spirit and leave us vulnerable and abandoned. The reality is that sometimes we are abused, and sometimes our feelings are just hurt, and we perceive it as abuse.

While that last statement might have made some of you want to rip up this curriculum and take offense, it must be emphasized that, regardless of the circumstances, a leader's responsibility is to love the sheep in their moments of struggle. The moment a leader beats the sheep in their struggle, it becomes abuse. The call on a leader is a high one, and it is a fine line that can easily be crossed if not for complete submission to the Spirit and the discipleship model of Jesus.

Personal Reflection:

Take a minute and review some of these common phrases associated with church hurt. Assess how these phrases make you feel when you hear them and discuss as a group why these phrases, even those that might have elements of truth, can be insensitive and also disruptive to the discipleship process of someone who has experienced church hurt or spiritual (or physical) abuse.

"Do not touch God's anointed."

"Don't forsake the assembly of the Saints."

"You just need to check your heart."

"If you leave this church, you are leaving God, you will be cursed, and you will not be anointed or blessed anymore."

"Pastors and leaders are human, too."

"If you don't like it, you can leave."

"Maybe the church is not the problem, maybe you're the problem."

"You just need to forgive and move on."

"You are just rebellious."

"She is just wounded and bitter and needs to handle her offense."

"The church didn't hurt you, you just don't like accountability."

"The church didn't hurt you, people hurt you."

"Everyone makes mistakes. Exposing ________ from a moment of weakness will ruin their ministry and make God look bad."

"When you don't forgive, you make God mad."

Before moving on, it must be emphasized that although these quotes make it seem like the church, its members, and its leaders are messed up and there is no hope, we can testify that good leaders DO exist. This curriculum exists to help guide those leaders. However, if you are a leader reading this, you may even think there have been times when you have demonstrated this behavior. **Be convicted but not condemned. Repent, do not relent!** Whether you have been the target or the source of spiritual abuse, God is in the business of redeeming and restoring your story. Forgiveness is a process, and restoration is a gift when possible. It is never too late to give it to Him, so be encouraged today to reap the full benefits of being discipled through the church.

Personal Reflection:

This could be the moment that the chains of offense, shame, hurt, or even sin could be broken off you from discipleship-gone-wrong. Do not miss this moment to allow the Lord to work in your heart, as this could be a moment of breakthrough. Pray for one another and allow the Spirit of God to move in your midst.

If you have carried the weight of offense from abuse in the church, choose forgiveness today.

If you have carried the weight of shame from abuse in the church, receive affirmation, love and truth from the Father today.

If the pain from abuse in the church has kept you from being in a relationship with the Lord, with the Church, or with the Christian community, may the Lord heal your heart with His love, free your mind with His truth, and revive your spirit to trust Him again and trust His Church once more.

LESSON 19 - CORPORATE EQUIPPING AND EDIFICATION

I, therefore, the prisoner of the Lord, beseech you to walk worthy of the calling with which you were called, with all lowliness and gentleness, with longsuffering, bearing with one another in love, endeavoring to keep the unity of the Spirit in the bond of peace. There is one body and one Spirit, just as you were called in one hope of your calling; one Lord, one faith, one baptism; one God and Father of all, who is above all, and through all, and in you all. However, to each one of us grace was given according to the measure of Christ's gift.

And He Himself gave some to be apostles, some prophets, some evangelists, and some pastors and teachers, for the equipping of the saints for the work of ministry, for the edifying of the body of Christ, till we all come to the unity of the faith and of the knowledge of the Son of God, to a perfect man, to the measure of the stature of the fullness of Christ; that we should no longer be children, tossed to and fro and carried about with every wind of doctrine, by the trickery of men, in the cunning craftiness of deceitful plotting, but, speaking the truth in love, may grow up in all things into Him who is the head—Christ— from whom the whole body, joined and knit together by what every joint supplies, according to the effective working by which every part does its share, causes growth of the body for the edifying of itself in love.

Ephesians 4 is now the pathway through which we zoom in to get more specific in what discipleship looks like, not just in our corporate Christian gathering, but in every level of discipleship. This excerpt of scripture reveals two essential "discipleship" phrases, **equipping** and **edification (building up)**. On one level, these seem easily understood, yet the extent of these meanings is rarely executed in discipleship or received well in discipleship. Let's see why.

To equip is **"to instruct or improve a person morally or intellectually."** To make disciples of Christ, we must look like Christ, which means we must improve morally. While this task is done easily and naturally in our friend groups and mentorship relationships, the truth is that edification should and does occur within the local church and can easily be attained through the T.E.A.M.S model.

Similarly, to edify means "to build up" or to promote another's growth in Christian wisdom, piety, happiness, and holiness. In Greek, this word is also used to describe the literal great structure or the building of a great structure.

This scripture supports the idea that to equip and edify the body of Christ adequately, corporate discipleship should include teaching, encouraging, advising, modeling, and serving. For any disciple to be edified and equipped, there must be a level of submission (as discussed in Chapter 1) that has developed from the established trust not just in church leadership but also in the congregation they are part of. The idea of submission was designed to aid edification and remind us of our eternal covenant with God. Jesus Himself claimed to be submitted to the Father and to serve. Jesus demonstrates perfect servant leadership as He discipled and interacted with people daily through constant submission and obedience to the Father, fulfilling servanthood's ultimate act by dying on the cross. Real leaders edify and equip the saints by themselves being submitted to the work of Christ, to other believers, and being sacrificial as they build up the body they are entrusted with. Our response to this should be honor, respect, and submission. This will flow into those who serve and attend the church, creating a healthy atmosphere of mutual edification and equipping for all believers.

Exploratory Scripture and Critical Thinking Exercise:

Read the following verses in connection with the Ephesians 4 passage from the beginning of this section and answer the questions below.

> *Have confidence in your leaders and submit to their authority, because they keep watch over you as those who must give an account. Do this so that their work will be a joy, not a burden, for that would be of no benefit to you. (Hebrews 10:17)*
>
> *All Scripture is inspired by God and is useful to teach us what is true and to make us realize what is wrong in our lives. It corrects us when we are wrong and teaches us to do what is right. God uses it to prepare and equip his people to do every good work. (2 Timothy 3:16-17)*
>
> *Each of you should use whatever gift you have received to serve others as faithful stewards of God's grace in its various forms. (1 Peter 4:10)*

Lesson 19 | Corporate Equipping and Edification

1. How do equipping and edification naturally happen in the church (consider all avenues, preaching, Sunday school, counseling, etc.)?

2. Are there opportunities to be equipped and edified that you are not taking advantage of?

3. What are some ways that the church, in general, could be more intentional about equipping and edifying its members through discipleship?

4. What opportunities do you see to equip and edify those around you? Is there a specific way you feel called to edify and equip in your local church?

LESSON 20 - DISCIPLESHIP IN CORPORATE GATHERINGS

Our corporate gatherings have various components. Jesus and the apostles established some, and men traditionally established others through denominations. Because all fundamental aspects of discipleship were ordained and established through Jesus, this curriculum will focus on how discipleship is found in our corporate gatherings through components mentioned explicitly in scripture.

As the components of the corporate gathering listed below are discussed regarding their relevance to discipleship, be mindful of the T.E.A.M.S. method. After each section, journal or consult with a small group or mentor about how the T.E.A.M.S method applies.

Singing

Ephesians 5:19 says to speak "to one another with psalms, hymns, and songs from the Spirit." The word translated to "speak" in Greek is λαλέω, which means to "speak or to preach." This means that when we sing corporately, we relay information about God to each other by ascribing His worth according to His excellent characteristics. Many people, especially new believers, formulate their theology and thoughts of God based on the lyrics in the songs they sing on Sunday mornings.

Teach

Encourage

Advise

Model

Serve

Prayer

In many churches across denominations, it is a part of the culture to pray scripture, much like the Jews. When we pray scripture, we are speaking out loud the promises of God, uplifting the body of Christ. In addition, corporate prayer, while general at times, is often prophetically inspired, through the truths of scripture, to petition God regarding His promises of healing, wisdom, protection, and provision that usually benefit the corporate gathering at large and uplift individuals. In addition, there is power in prayer. Jesus teaches that when "two or more are gathered," there is power in their declarations and unity.

> *Again, I say to you, if two of you agree on earth about anything they ask, my Father in heaven will do it for them. For where two or three are gathered in my name, there am I among them.* (Matthew 18:19-20)

Lesson 20 | Discipleship in Corporate Gatherings

Teach

Encourage

Advise

Model

Serve

Preaching and Teaching

Declaring the word of God to the people of God is what preachers do! When someone gets up to preach, their number one goal is to remind or reveal to the people of God the promises of God and the love of God through the truth found in scripture. Teaching is built in naturally to preaching. When someone preaches, they often declare things that are not otherwise known or give information that might explain how to do or accomplish something with instructions, using the Word of God as the primary source. The point of teaching is not for the teacher to do it for the student but for the student to learn to do it independently. However, so many people come to hear the preaching on Sunday mornings and don't intentionally apply it to their lives throughout the week. They are missing out on an opportunity to be discipled; how sad!

> *In the presence of God and of Christ Jesus, who will judge the living and the dead, and given His appearing□and His kingdom, I give you this charge: 2 Preach□the word; be prepared in season and out of season; correct, rebuke and encourage—with great patience and careful instruction.* (2 Timothy 4:1-2)

Teach

Encourage

Advise

Model

Serve

Baptism

Water baptism is not the avenue by which we are saved, but it is symbolic and an essential part of our public declaration of Jesus Christ as Lord of our lives. Jesus ties baptism directly to discipleship in His famous "Great Commission."

> *In the presence of God and of Christ Jesus, who will judge the living and the dead, and given His appearing and His kingdom, I give you this charge: Preach the word; be prepared in season and out of season; correct, rebuke and encourage with great patience and careful instruction*. (Matthew 28:19-20.)

This public declaration should be essential for the individual believer's life and the corporate body they belong to. When someone is baptized, the corporate body should rally around that person, committing to them as brothers and sisters in Christ to unite and disciple one another.

Teach

Encourage

Advise

Model

Serve

Communion

Jesus sat with His disciples and broke bread, initiating the ordinance of communion as His last interaction with them before being handed over to the dead. At this moment, He was preparing them for what was about to happen, and Jesus also fully revealed Himself as Lord and Savior to His disciples. He was not only preparing them for what was about to happen, but they had to write to the Corinthian church to remember that the point of communion is not to party or indulge but to remember the death of the Lord Jesus Christ as a corporate unit. What a beautiful privilege to honor our Lord Jesus by recalling His death with the body of Christ.

Teach

Encourage

Advise

Model

Serve

Fellowship and Service

American church culture looks quite different than church culture in most other countries, but it certainly looks different than the early church. Like in the early church, in many other countries, when believers gather corporately, it is more than just a two-hour event; it is an "all-day" event and, in some instances, a real community that participates in most aspects of life together. At the least, our corporate gatherings on Sunday morning should include plenty of opportunities to talk over coffee or a pastry, sit and catch up, or pray with one another. At most, we should be together throughout the week, serving and loving one another like family. It should be normative for us to call up our pastors to discuss a decision we need to make and feel like we are talking to our brother in Christ, who has our best interests at heart. It should be normative for us to go in droves out to a restaurant after dinner on Sunday afternoons simply because we desire the fellowship of the body of Christ. It should be normative for us to serve one another and fill in the gaps spiritually and physically in fellowship for one another.

Teach

Encourage

Lesson 20 | Discipleship in Corporate Gatherings

Advise

Model

Serve

Practical Application:

As you've gone through these areas of discipleship that occur as the Church gathers, which of these has served to "disciple" you most? Remember, even for those of us not on the stage, the Lord can use us in the pews to disciple other believers around us! How does our demeanor or posture as we participate in corporate worship disciple those around us? How does our heart posture and demeanor minister to others in the body of Christ?"

LESSON 21 - ATTEND AND JOIN A LOCAL CHURCH

This section has likely stirred up some things inside of each of us. Some may be excited to view their corporate church experience from this new perspective of seeing discipleship in every aspect and want to attend church more often. Others may be disappointed that there may be elements missing in their experiences. Some may now understand their hesitancy to attend church because of the abuses mentioned in this chapter. However, cliché it might sound, it is true that the Church is not perfect, and not just any church is where God wants YOU to be. While all churches are called to disciple, each has specific mandates and purposes. We would suggest that you consider the following before committing to join in unity with members of a particular church body:

1. Is this church preaching the truth of the Gospel message as evidenced in the Word from a balanced perspective?

2. Do I sense community and unity among the church members related to the purpose of this church?

3. Do I feel encouraged yet challenged and convicted to grow in my walk with the Lord?

4. Are the leaders not just preaching truth but also modeling it in their interactions with others in and out of the church?

5. Is the leadership accessible?

6. Are there ways for me to serve, be equipped, and be edified?

7. Did God call me here?

If you can answer these questions positively, you are likely in the right place! Red flags are often related to anything that is false gospel or even anti-God. Just because a church doesn't have every program you can think of doesn't mean it isn't the church for you.

Here are a few characteristics of a healthy church that can help you be grateful for your church, pray for your church, or wait upon the Lord to find the right church for you:

1.Healthy churches have plurality in leadership. This means that no man or woman is calling all of the shots without discussing or carrying the weight of the entire congregation on his/her shoulders. Depending on denominational beliefs, this could look like a team of elders and deacons, a team of teaching pastors, a team of leaders established in specific five-fold offices according to Ephesians 4, etc.)

2.Healthy churches have leadership submitted to a board and/or a denominational/ministry covering comprised of mothers and fathers in the faith.

3.Healthy churches have a variety of vetted/high-quality teachers appearing in the pulpit.

4.Healthy churches have tangible signs of the fruit of the Spirit on display in the congregation members (a sign of spiritual growth and maturity attained through discipleship).

Questions for Discussion:

1. What drew you to the church you are currently in?

2. What has inspired you to stay?

3. What markers of a healthy church do you see in your church body?

4. Have you asked the Lord to guide you to the church home he has for you?

Personal Reflection:

This section can be easy to breeze past, especially if you already belong to a church, but the truth is that many of us end up at the church we are at for reasons that are not spirit-filled, but fleshly satisfied. This word may sound harsh, but sometimes the problem isn't the church; sometimes it is us. Take the time to evaluate why you attend the church you attend. Resist doing this with a critical spirit, but instead with a submissive heart posture. If the Lord confirms why you are where you are, what are you waiting for? Dive in! Get connected! Serve your local church. Make friends, get a community, and most of all, pray for your local leaders. Do not just be a bench warmer; it's time for you to get into the game.

ABOUT THE REAL MOVEMENT

The Real Movement is a faith-based, multi-denominational community that supports young adult women by addressing the real issues they face in today's culture, fostering a safe environment, and studying Scripture. Their events and resources for young women and their leaders promote honest, healthy conversations about topics such as singleness, dating, anxiety, depression, fear, abortion, physical and sexual assault, purity culture, sexual sin, social media, labels, eating disorders, and more. This curriculum was created by women involved in the Real Movement, aiming to help women learn how to build a Christian community as a support system from a Biblical perspective.

---

www.ingramcontent.com/pod-product-compliance
Lightning Source LLC
LaVergne TN
LVHW081324110826
845149LV00007B/1591

* 9 7 8 1 9 6 1 9 8 3 0 3 8 *